KNOCKABOUT

The Pen is Mightier Than the Word ©2018
by Martin Rowson.

Published by Knockabout Ltd. 42c Lancaster Road,
London W11 1QR, United Kingdom.

Martin Rowson has asserted his rights under the
Copyright, Designs and Patents Act 1988 to be
identified as the author of this work.

All rights reserved. No part of this book may be
reproduced, stored in a retrieval system or transmitted
in any form without the prior permission of the
publisher or copyright holder.

"Creation" originally appeared in *Black Eye III*.
"Lost Books", "Plucked", "Despair", "Decay" & "Soul"
all originally appeared in successive editions of
The Seagull Catalogue. "Gluttony" was originally published
in the anthology *The Seven Deadly Sins*.

A CIP catalogue record for this book is available from the
British Library.

ISBN 9780861662647

Printed in China.

In memory of Nick Priestland, restaurateur, cook, gardener, artist, hotelier, conversationalist and host; with thanks to Naveen Kishore, who browbeat me into creating, wholly philanthropically, a lot of what follows; and, as ever, with all my love, for Anna, Fred & Rose.

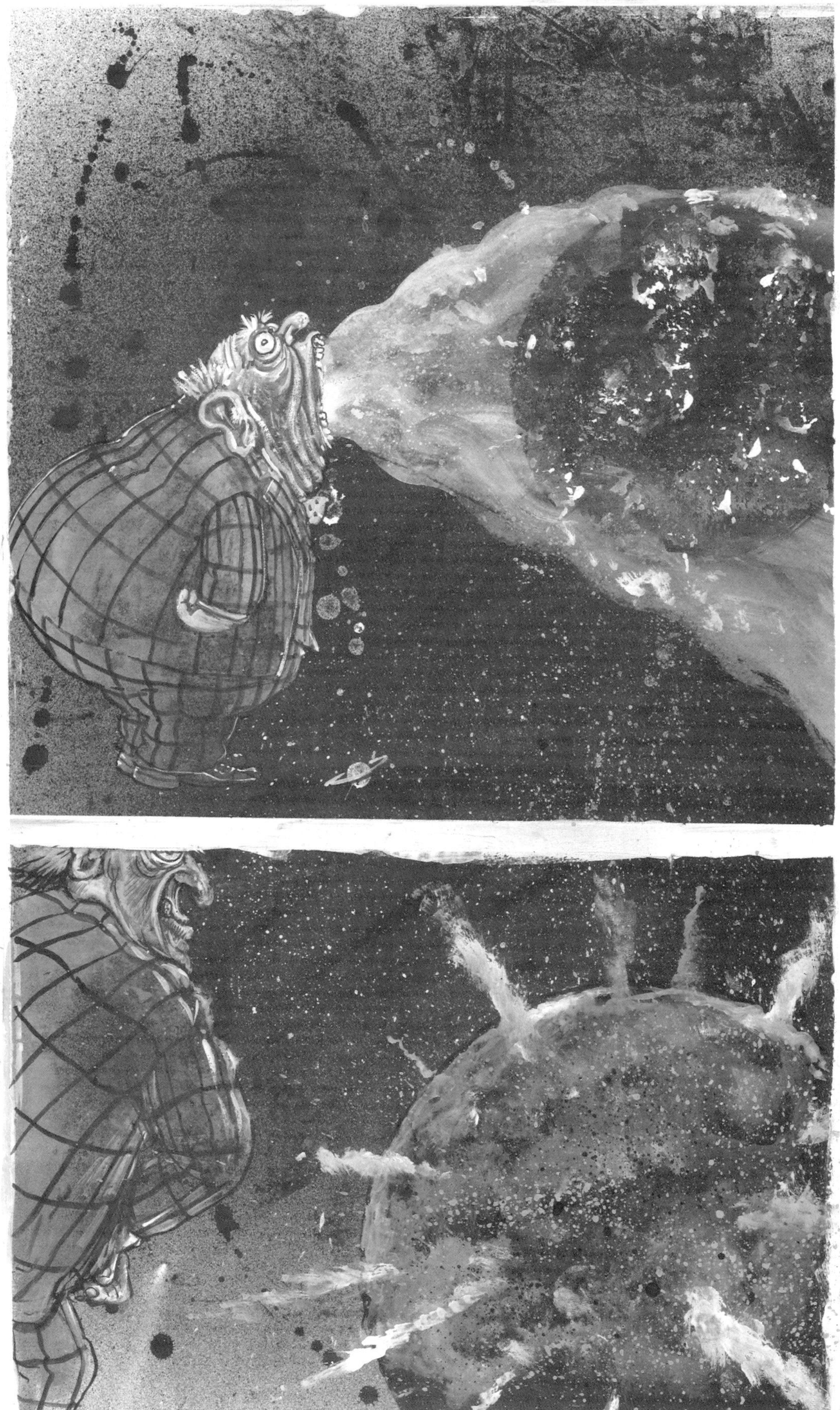

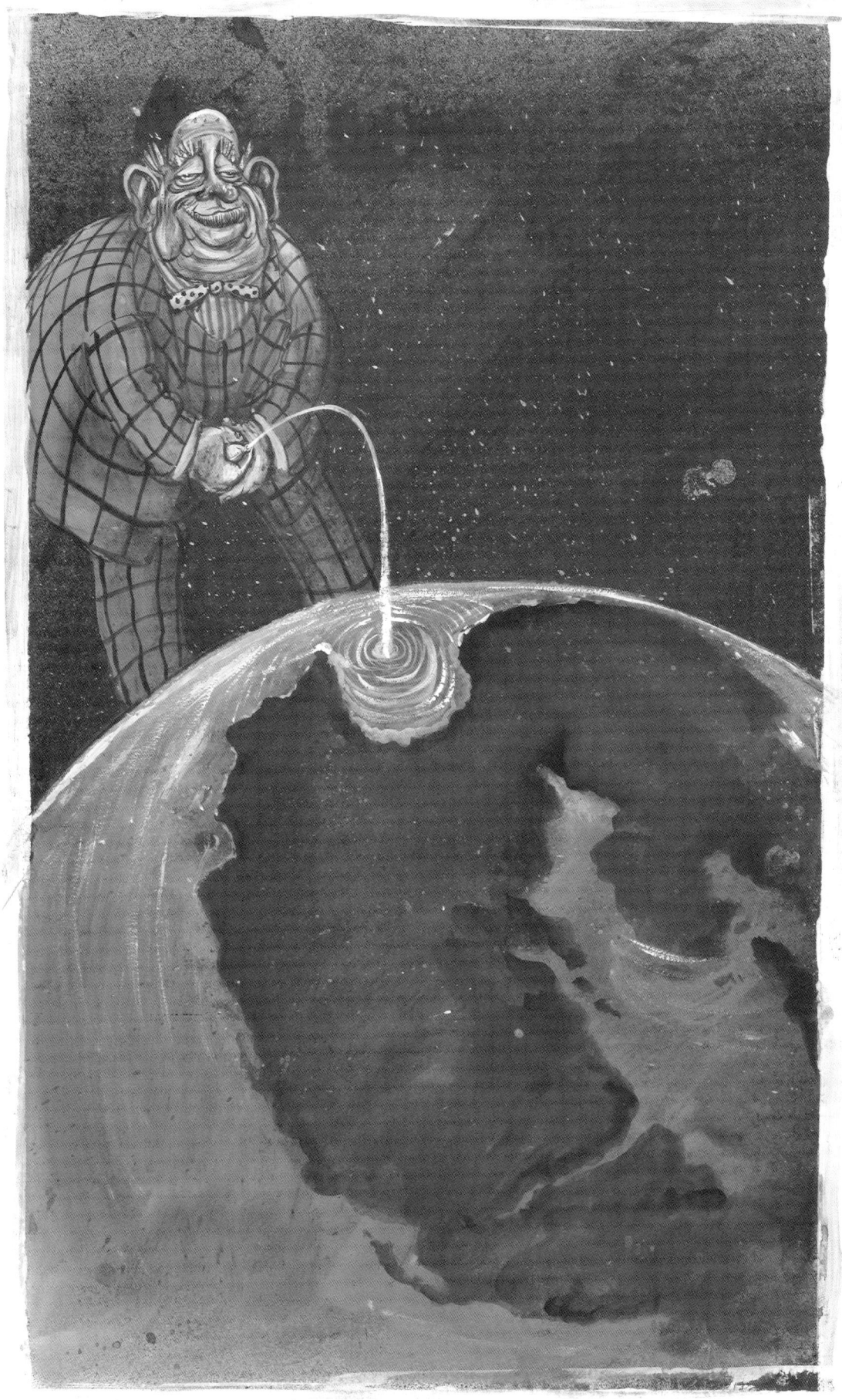

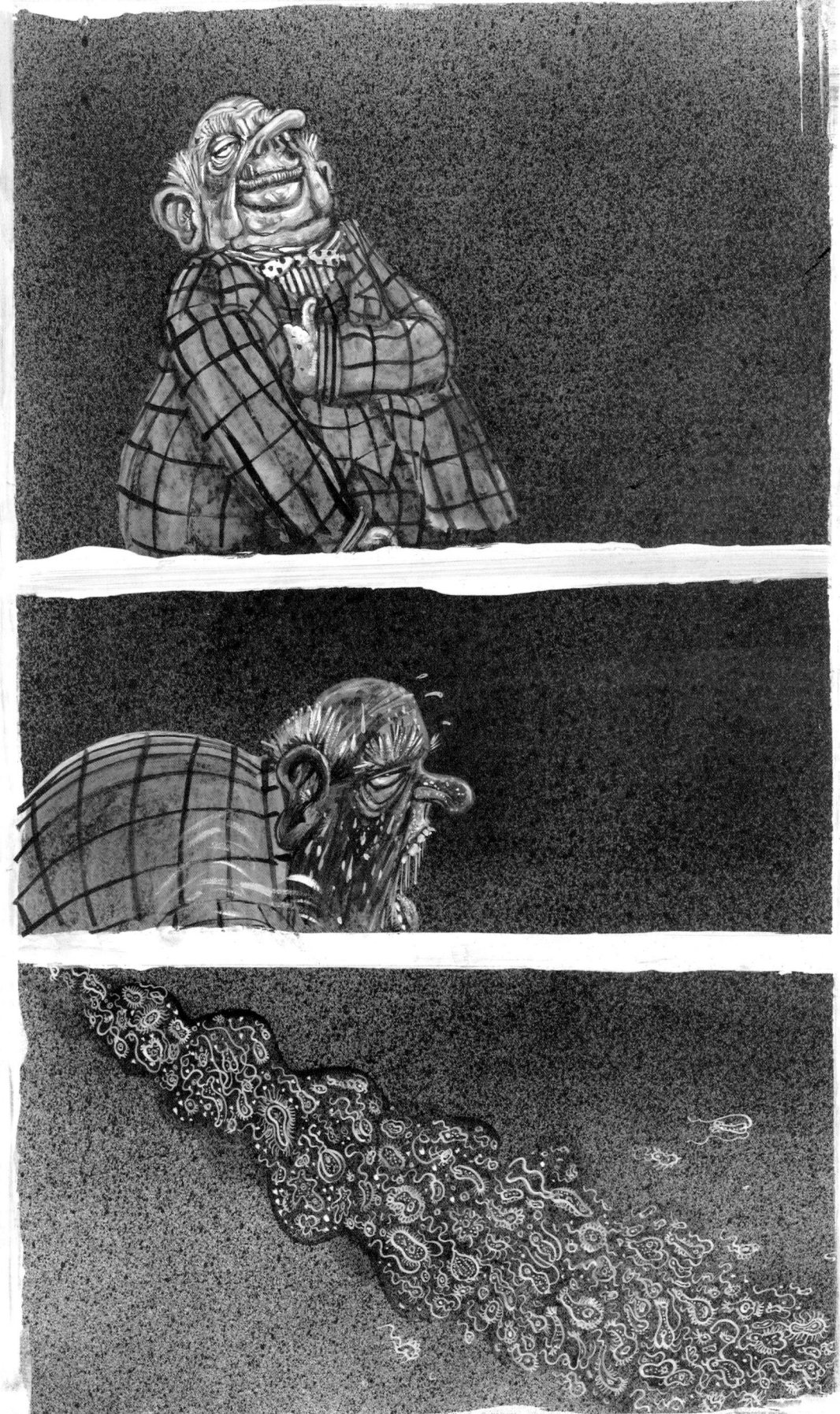

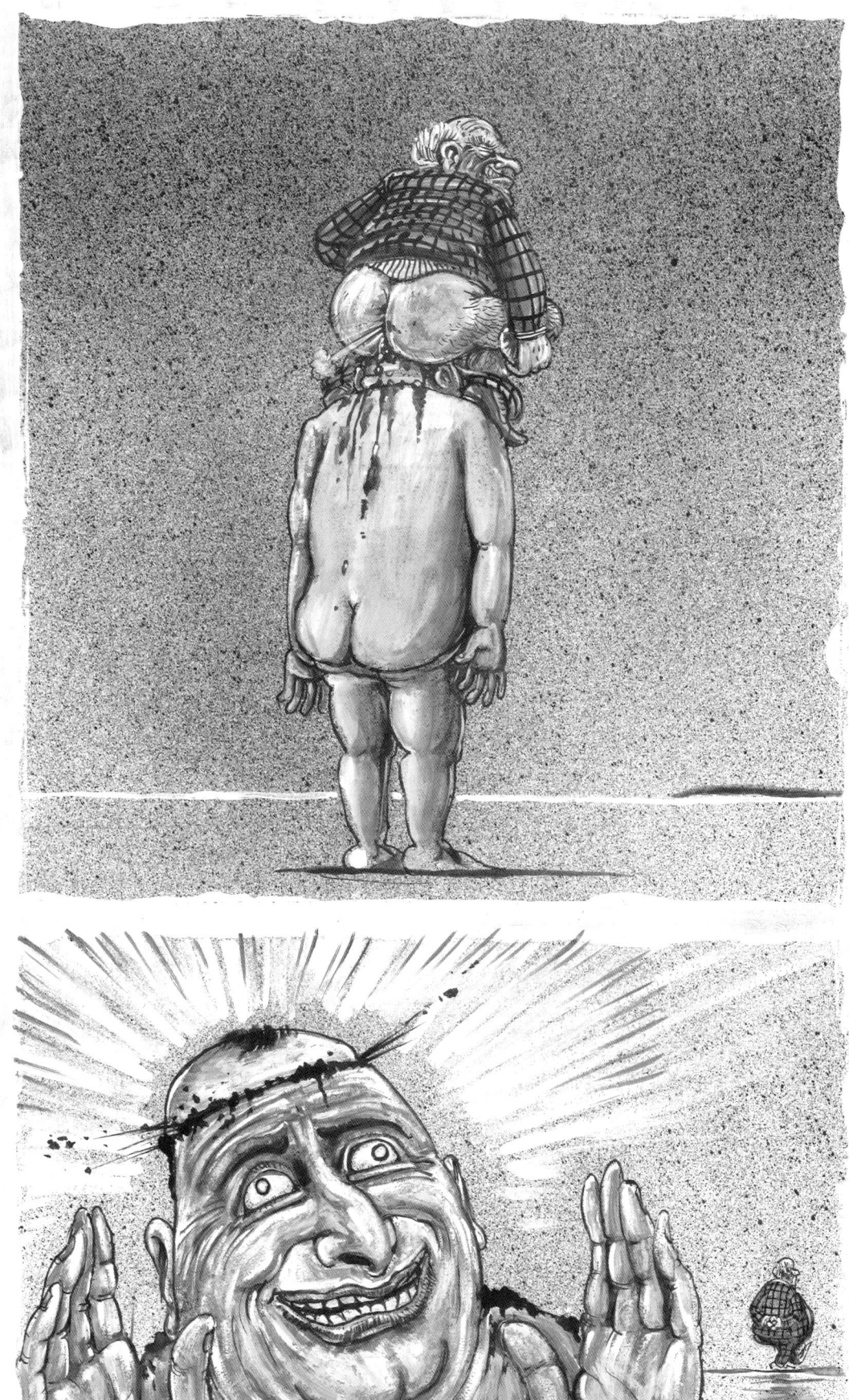

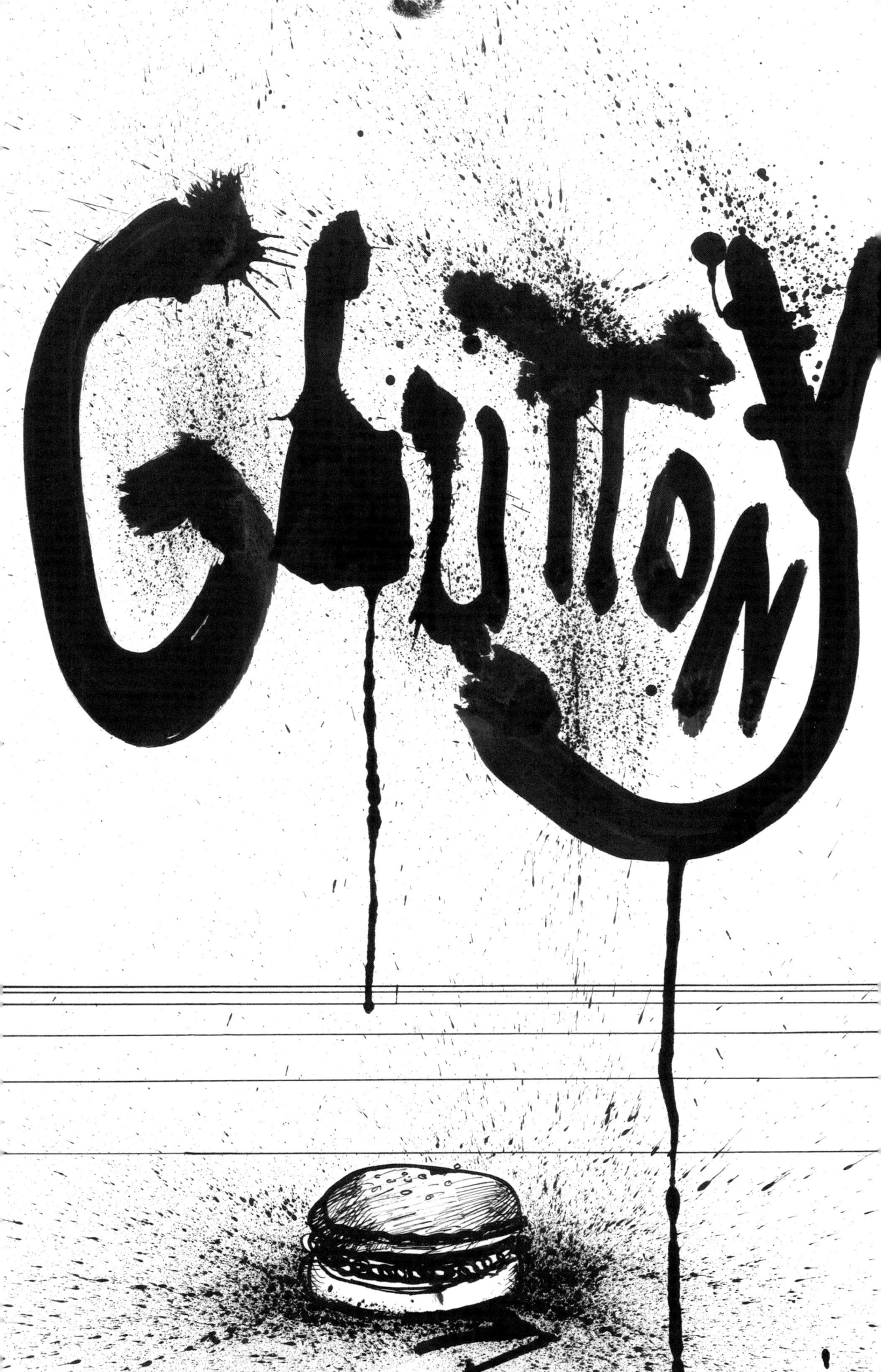

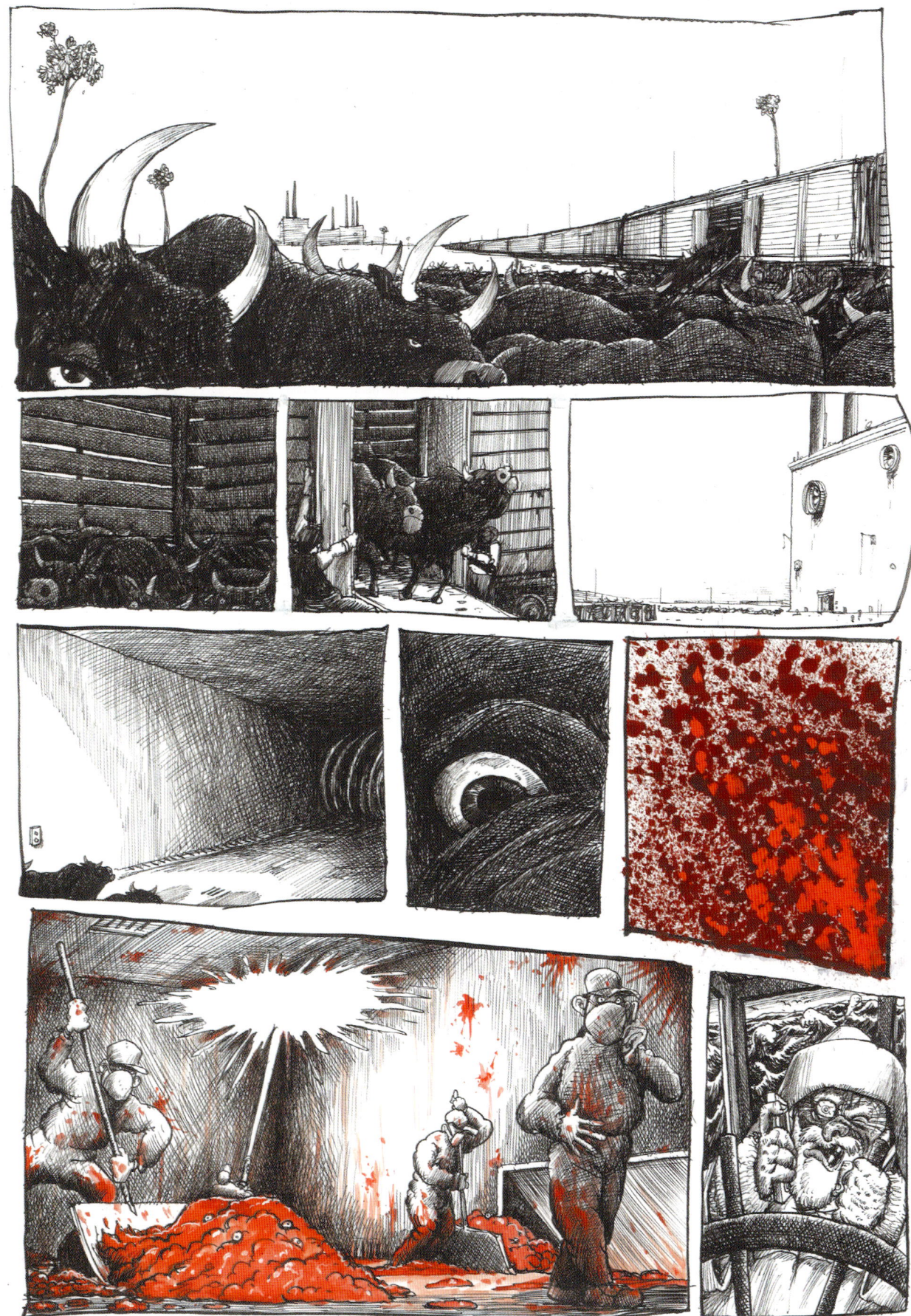

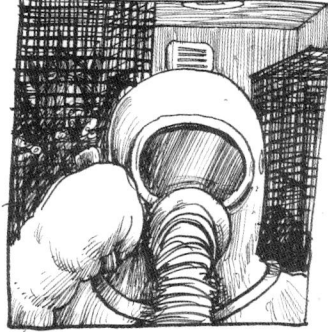

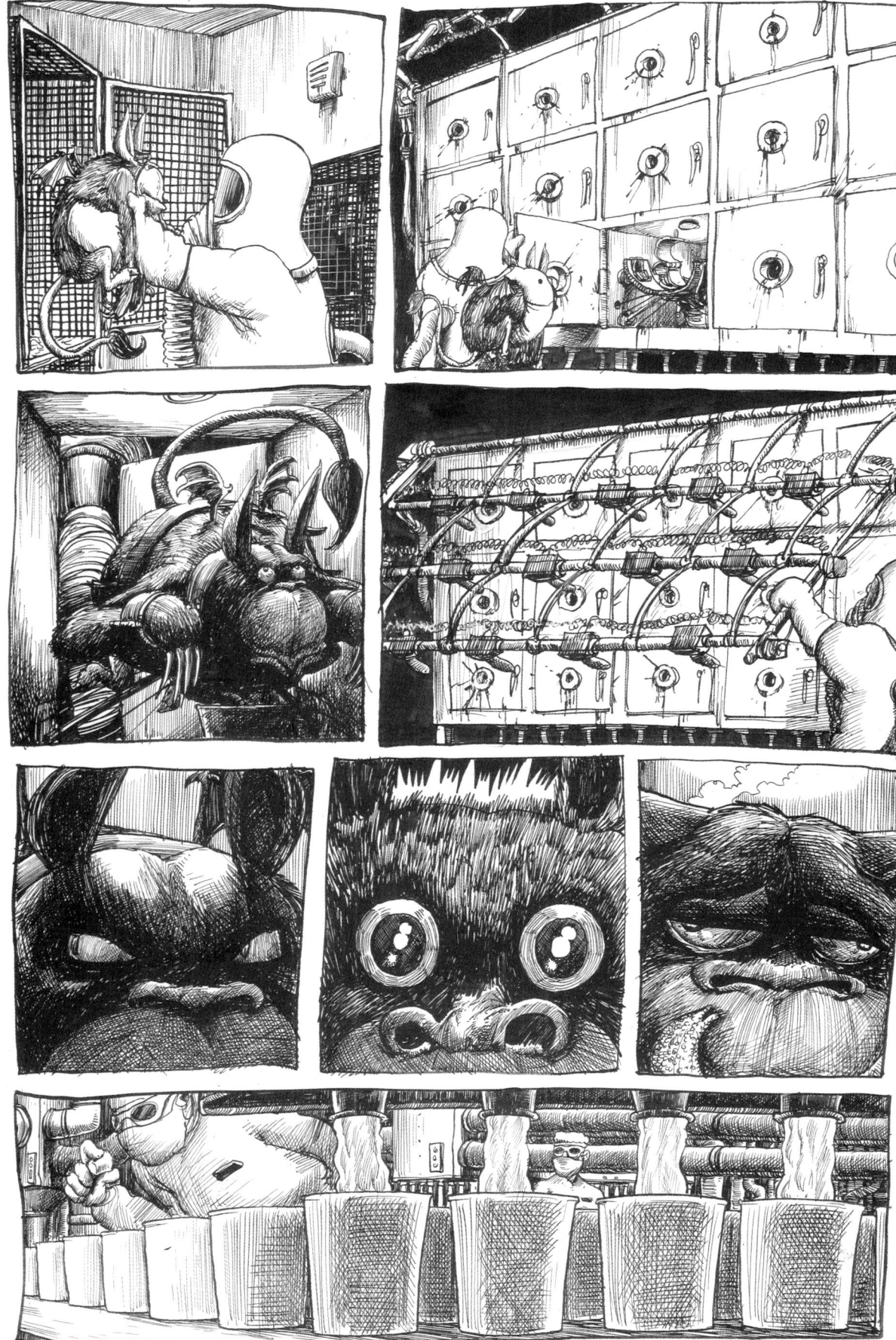

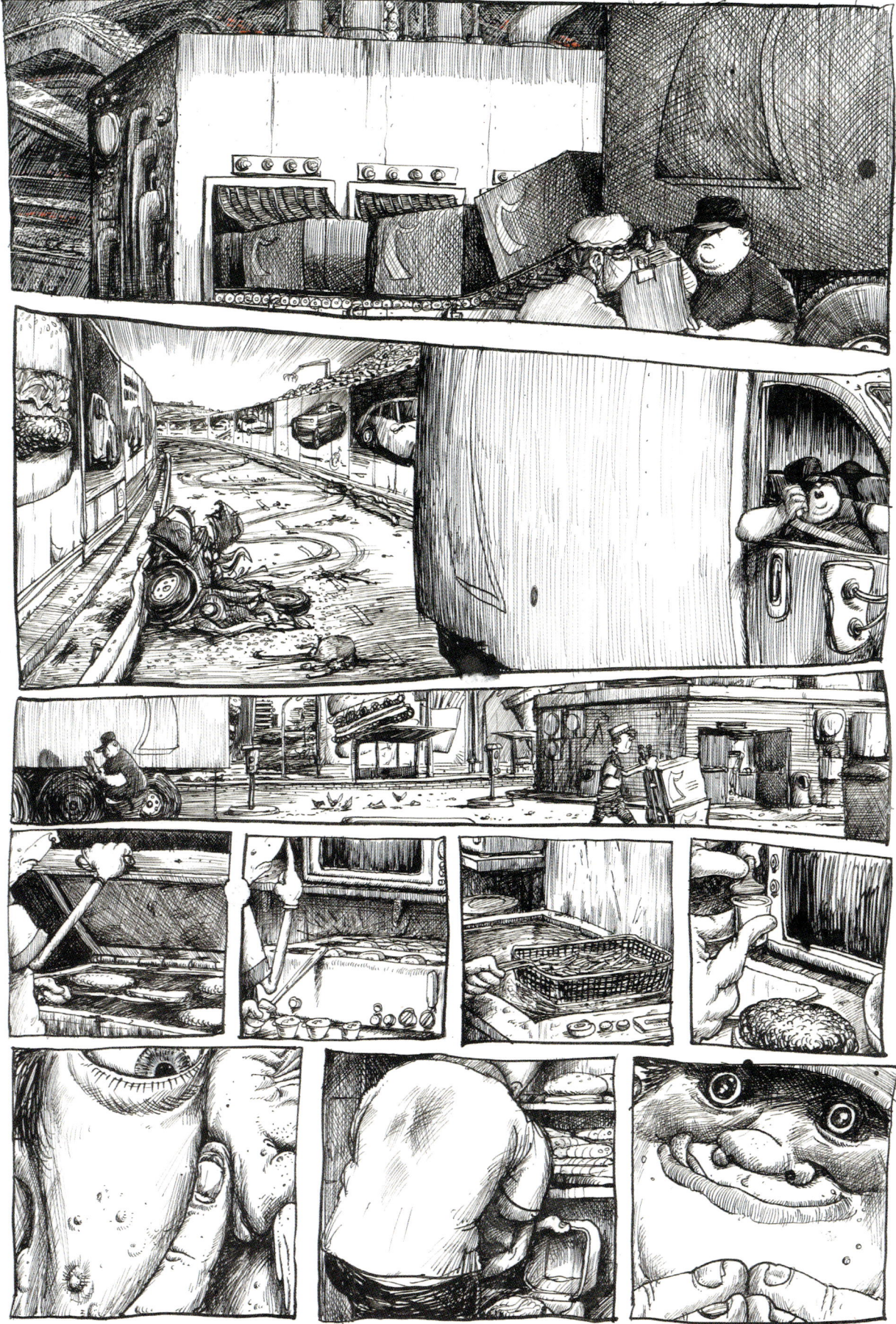

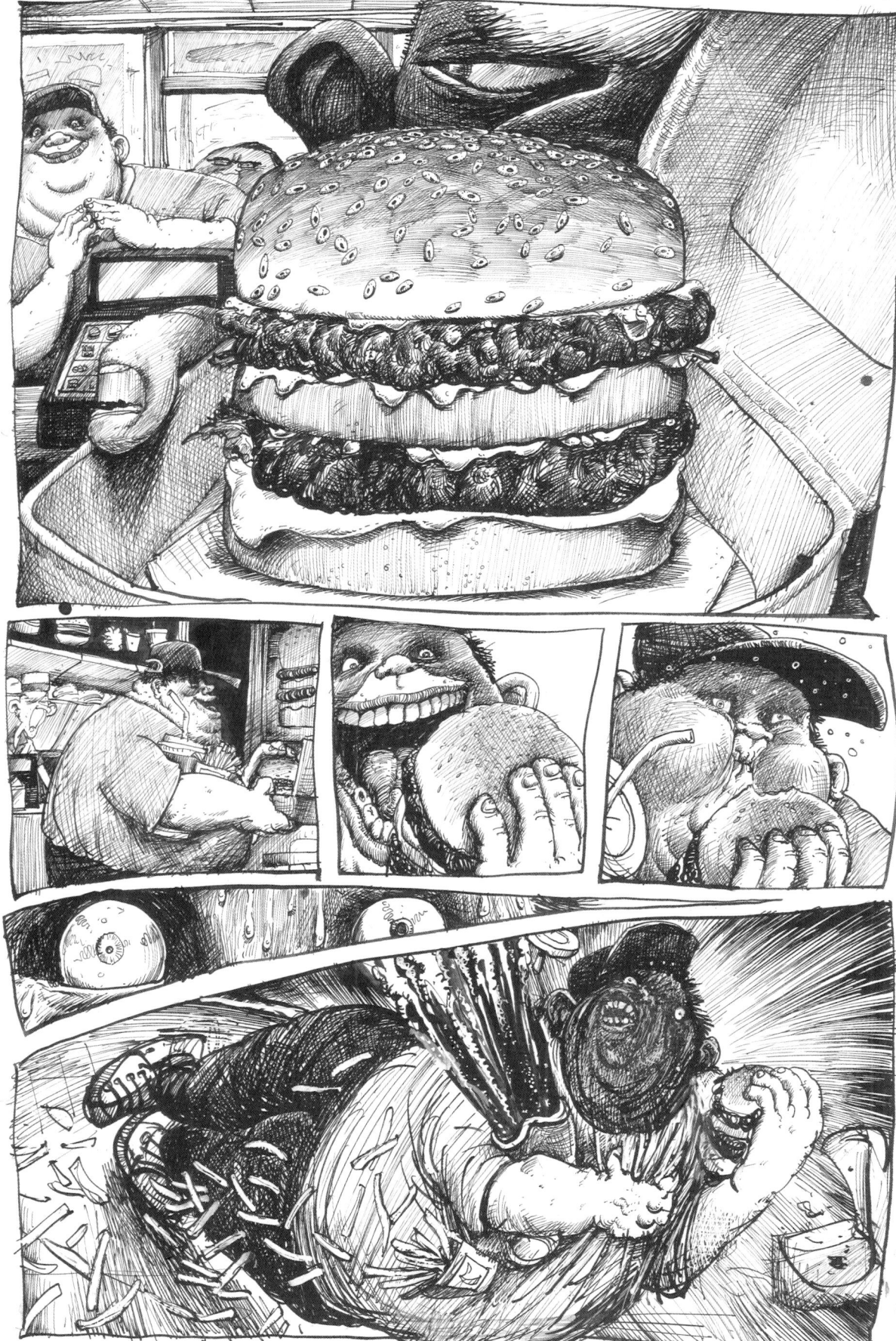

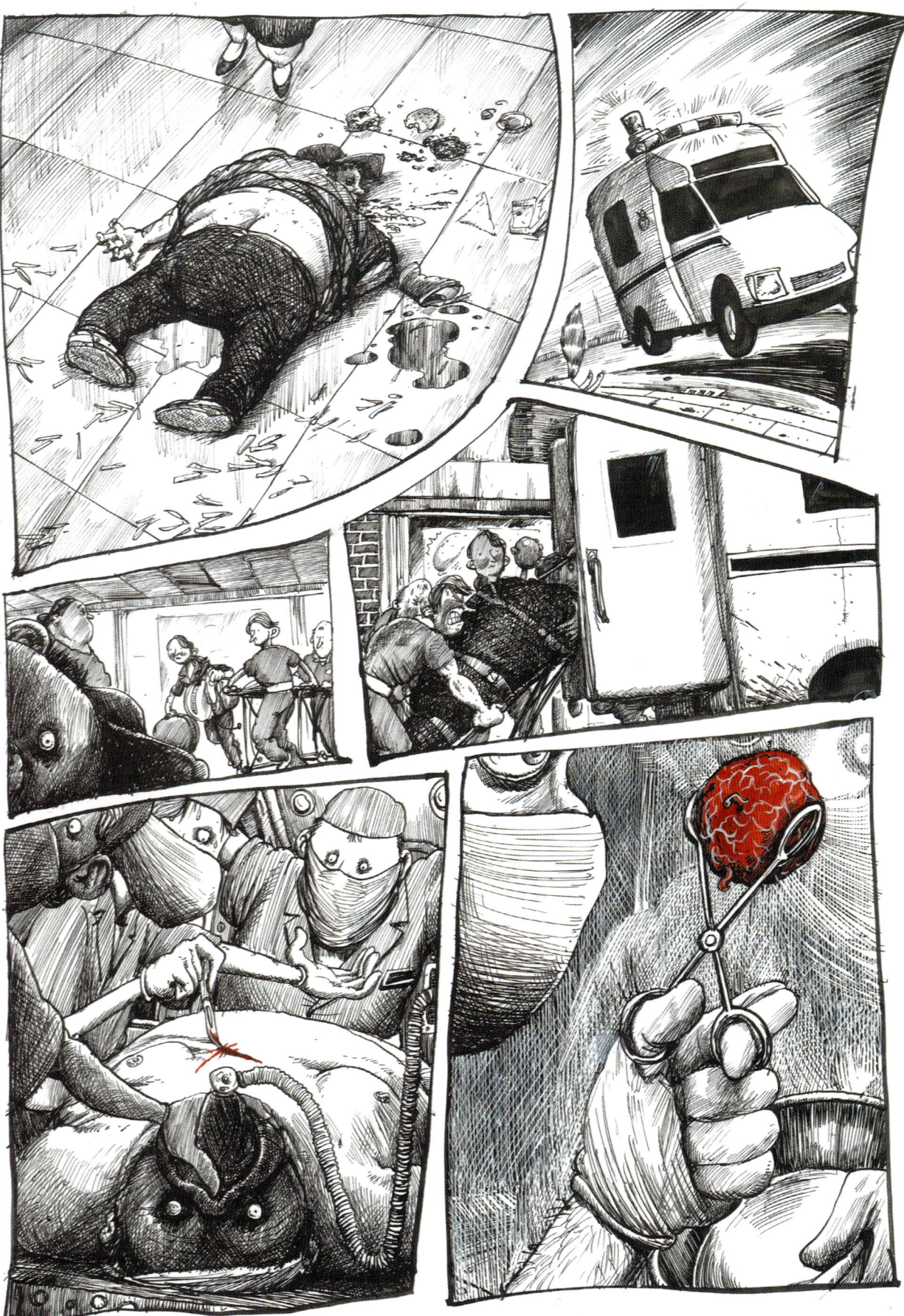

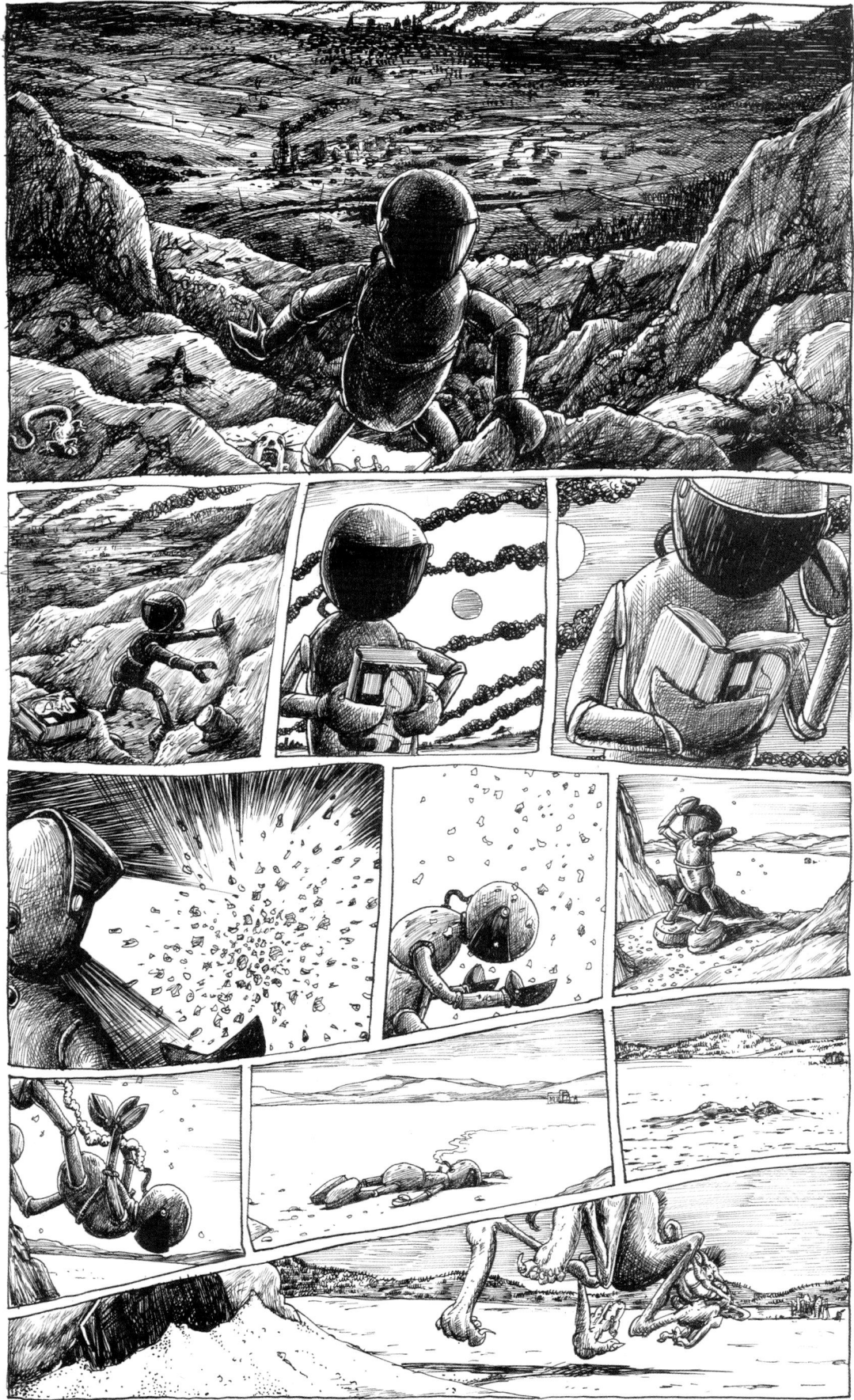

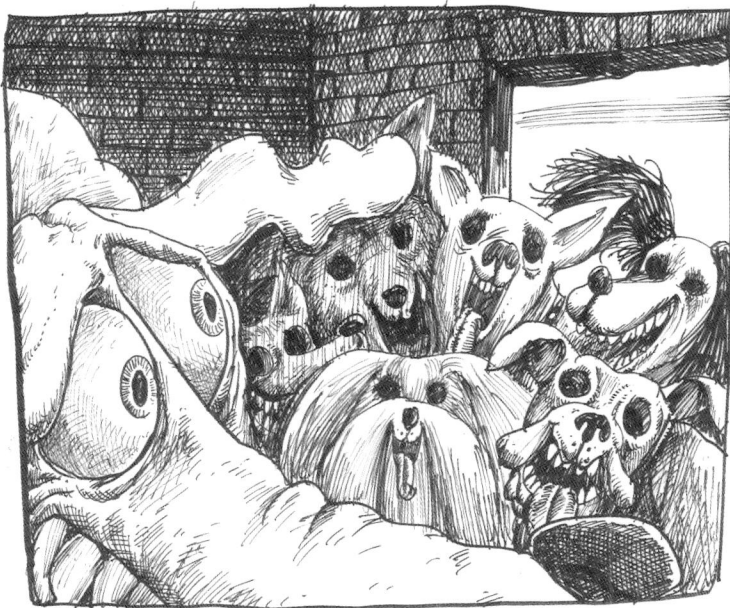

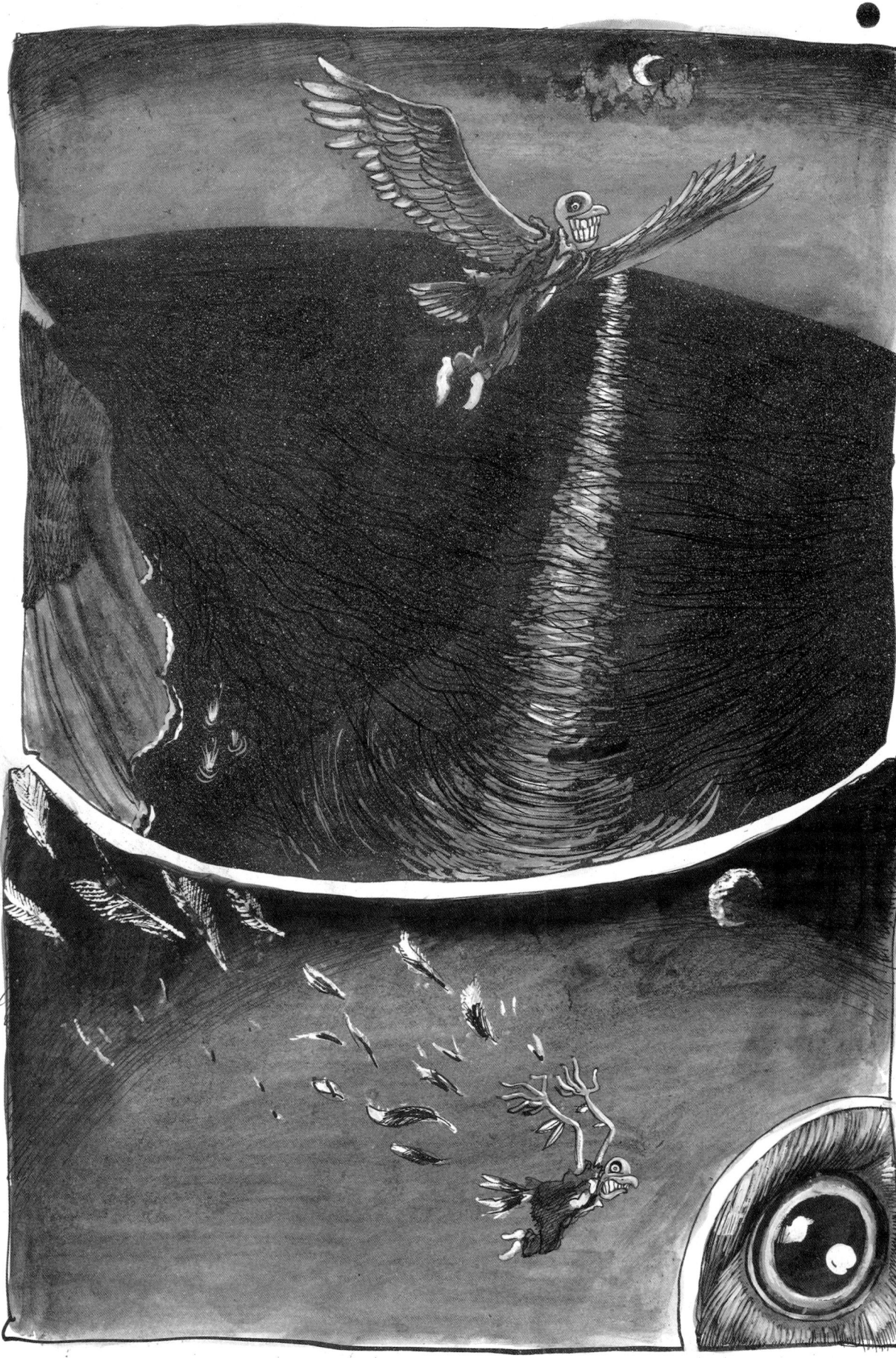